FAIR PARK

Carlo Ciampaglia was one of the primary muralists invited to Dallas by George Dahl to create artwork for the Texas Centennial Exposition in 1936. The artist was responsible for the large-scale murals on the Hall of Transportation, including *Transportation of the Future*, seen in this image. Two stylized and muscular figures escort a Jules Vernian rocket ship into outer space. This was one of the earliest depictions of space flight on a monumental public mural in the United States. (Courtesy of the Dallas Municipal Archives.)

ON THE FRONT COVER: The Texas Centennial Exposition of 1936 was the third world's fair staged in America during the 1930s. The centerpiece of the exposition was the Esplanade of State, a 700-foot-long reflecting pool flanked by monumental buildings, sculpture, and flags that symbolized the six nations that ruled Texas since its discovery by Spanish explorers in 1540. The visual terminus of the esplanade was the majestic State of Texas Building, which was placed on a raised terrace to command the attention of visitors to the fair. At night, the buildings and artwork along the esplanade were dramatically lit, and the entire ensemble was transformed into an ethereal vision by a bank of 24 powerful searchlights radiating from behind the State of Texas Building. (Courtesy of the State Fair of Texas Archives.)

ON THE BACK COVER: Visitors to the State Fair of Texas in 1903 encountered this ensemble of buildings at the Parry Avenue entrance to Fair Park. The structure to the left in this image is the main gate to the fair, built in 1886, where tickets were purchased and pedestrians entered the fairgrounds. The structure to the right is the fair's administration building, which was added in the 1890s. In this view, fair visitors await the trolleys that provided transportation between Fair Park and downtown Dallas. (Courtesy of the Texas/Dallas History and Archives Division, Dallas Public Library.)

FAIR PARK

WILLIS CECIL WINTERS

Published by Arcadia Publishing
Charleston SC, Chicago IL, Portsmouth NH, San Francisco CA

Printed in the United States of America

Library of Congress Control Number: 2010927857

For all general information contact Arcadia Publishing at:
Telephone 843-853-2070
Fax 843-853-0044
E-mail sales@arcadiapublishing.com
For customer service and orders:
Toll-Free 1-888-313-2665

Visit us on the Internet at www.arcadiapublishing.com

This book is dedicated to the staff of the Dallas Park and Recreation Department in recognition of their passionate and devoted stewardship of a national historic landmark.

CONTENTS

Acknowledgments   6

Introduction   7

1.   The Grand Venture   9

2.   The Great State Fair   21

3.   From State Fair to World's Fair   53

4.   The Year America Discovered Dallas   67

5.   The Art of the Exposition   129

6.   Fair Park Today   139

Select Bibliography   143

ACKNOWLEDGMENTS

I want to express my profound appreciation to Sally Rodriguez for her very hard work in helping me identify the images for this book over a short span of time. Sally was responsible for all the coordination with the various archives and other sources of photographs and for keeping things organized along the way. This was a monumental task for which I am very grateful. I am also grateful to Errol McKoy at the State Fair of Texas for making the archives available to us, and to Sue Gooding for her patient assistance as we went through the incredible collection of images. Special thanks also go to Susan Richardson at the Dallas Historical Society for granting us access to its treasures of the Texas Centennial Exposition. John Slate, in the Dallas Municipal Archives, was extremely helpful not only in bending over backwards to provide us with great images, but also in assisting me with dating a few of the photographs. Carol Roark and Rachel Howell in the Texas/Dallas History and Archives Division at the Dallas Public Library were both extremely responsive—as always—and of great assistance in allowing me access to their tremendous collections. I also appreciate the assistance of Louise Elam in the Dallas Park and Recreation Department for helping us secure images of the restored buildings and artwork at Fair Park from various sources. A final note of thanks to all our consultants and friends not mentioned above for providing us with photographs of their fine work.

INTRODUCTION

From its auspicious inauguration in 1886 on the site that would later become known as Fair Park, Dallas's state fair has been inextricably linked with the city's emergence as the agricultural and commercial capital of North Texas. The site selected for this grand venture was a flat prairie east of Dallas, utterly featureless but for the occasional tree, tracks of the Texas and Pacific Railroad, and cotton fields that stretched to the horizon. It was a bold undertaking and risky investment to be sure: the capitalization and sustenance of a fair that presumed to embody the aspirations of a state the size of Texas. The fair's founding fathers were the city's business elite, however, who were not disposed to failure. By the 1880s, there was an aura of optimism and invincibility that permeated the city's mercantile, banking, and manufacturing establishment. This culture of entrepreneurial success nurtured the fair through a long period of incubation and through alternating episodes of catastrophe and expansion, which required additional capital, new investment, and always more land. If the acquisition of two crossing railroad lines 14 years earlier had propelled Dallas on a trajectory that would establish its economic dominion over North Texas, the state fair would ultimately solidify the city's reputation and prowess as a center of commerce, trade, and agriculture for the region. Fair Park's growth and development as a cultural center would come a little later.

As Dallas grew, the state fair grew along with it. In 1900, there were 42,600 residents in the city, making it the second largest in the state. Within two decades the population would increase fourfold, and Fair Park would begin to assume a role more vital to Dallas than that of an annual agricultural fair. It became a year-round park and destination. Facilities and venues essential to Dallas's aspirations as a center of education and culture were constructed on the fairgrounds—including an auditorium, an art museum, and a coliseum. More and larger structures were added at a dizzying pace. As the 1920s drew to a close, Fair Park was almost completely built out, with little room for expansion. The fairgrounds needed a new catalyst for growth, and an opportunity would soon be presented by the coming world's fair.

Fair Park was the nucleus of Dallas's bid to host the 1936 Texas Centennial Exposition. Its impressive campus of exhibition buildings and entertainment venues was unmatched by that in any other city in the state. Over the course of 50 years, Fair Park had developed from its humble origins of wooden Victorian-era buildings, all gradually replaced by more permanent steel and masonry edifices. The responsibility of transforming this collection of buildings into a world's fair fell upon the shoulders of George Dahl, a Dallas architect who assisted the powerful banker R. L. Thornton in securing the exposition for their hometown. Staging the exposition, however, was an ambitious undertaking for a city of 260,000 still in the throes of the Great Depression. But the fair's organizers were up to the task.

A talented team of architects and artists was assembled to design the layout and new buildings for the exposition. A plan for an expanded Fair Park was developed that integrated and altered the existing structures of the fairgrounds. Monumental vistas, modernistic buildings, landscaping, and lighting miraculously transformed Fair Park into an exposition that celebrated the 100th anniversary of Texas' independence from Mexico.

Today Fair Park is the largest intact exposition site and one of the largest collections of art deco architecture remaining in the United States. With its 26 extant buildings from the Centennial, Fair Park was named a national historic landmark in 1986. Long neglected, its buildings deteriorating, and its art obscured and forgotten, the park's future seemed uncertain until the early 1990s, when the city of Dallas, with assistance from the private sector, implemented a comprehensive plan to restore the structures and conserve the artwork.

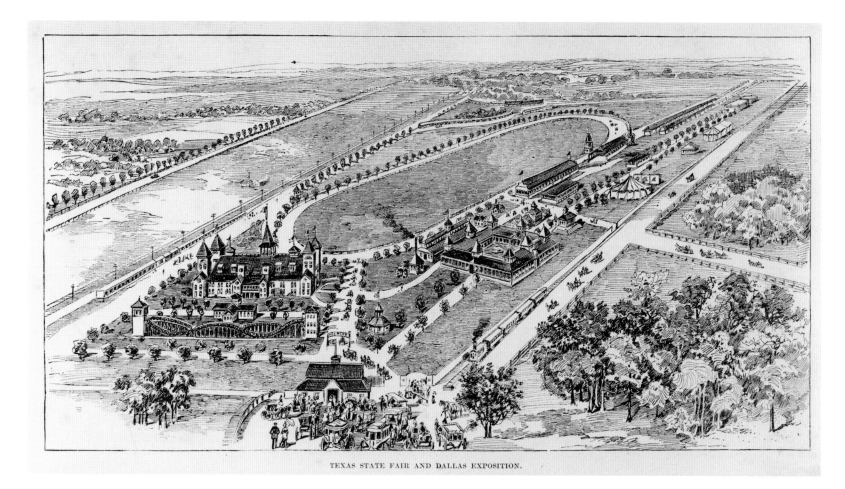

TEXAS STATE FAIR AND DALLAS EXPOSITION.

This aerial pictorial view was published in *Frank Leslie's Illustrated Newspaper* in 1890. The fairgrounds were laid out on an 80-acre tract of land in the cotton fields east of Dallas, and the Dallas State Fair and Exposition was held on this site in 1886. The principal features of the fair, evident in this view, included a 1-mile racetrack with grandstand seating for 8,000, the main Exposition Building, Machinery Hall, and an amusement zone with restaurants. As the fair grew and developed over the ensuing 50 years, there would be little change from this early arrangement of streets and axes as well as the locations of the principal buildings. (Courtesy of the Dallas Historical Society Archives.)

OPPOSITE: The main Exposition Building (seen at left) was the most imposing structure on the fairgrounds from 1886 until it burned to the ground in 1902. Measuring 200 feet by 300 feet, with corner towers over 100 feet in height, this massive wooden structure was designed by James Flanders, the first professional architect in Dallas. The building featured a ladies department and exhibits on education, art, horticulture, and geology. In 1890, a Music Hall seating 2,500 (at right), also designed by Flanders, was constructed on the northeast corner of the Exposition Building. A gallery stretching across the third floor had excellent views of the races held on the nearby track. Inside the auditorium, an organ with 3,000 pipes was installed by the Louisville, Kentucky, organ builder, Henry Pilcher and Sons. (Courtesy of the State Fair of Texas Archives.)

ONE

THE GRAND VENTURE

The foundations of the present state fair were laid in 1886 with the charter of the Dallas State Fair and Exposition. An 80-acre site was purchased east of Dallas in an area described by rival interests as "the worst kind of hog wallow." The initial layout of the fairgrounds consisted of a racetrack occupying the center of the site with tree-lined promenades to the south and west. Two major Victorian-era exhibit structures, including the immense Exposition Building and the smaller Machinery Hall, were constructed, in addition to an entrance gate, grandstands for the track, livestock barns, and other smaller structures.

A rival fair in Dallas was also held in 1886, and although the two events were each modestly successful, organizers saw the futility of competition and joined forces to reincorporate as the Texas State Fair and Dallas Exposition the following year at the East Dallas site. More investments and improvements were made at the fairgrounds, and the state fair managed to survive the economic recession of the 1890s before a series of cataclysmic events struck that caused financial difficulty. Over a period of several years, fires struck the wooden exhibit structures on the fairgrounds, culminating with the destruction of the main exhibition building

in 1902. A second disaster occurred the following year when the state outlawed track gambling, which was the fair's primary source of revenue. Facing financial oblivion, the fair association negotiated an agreement with the City of Dallas. In exchange for liquidating the association's debts, the directors deeded the fairgrounds to the city, and both parties shared in the cost of building a new, fireproof exhibit hall. The city would own and maintain the fairgrounds as a public park and turn the site over to the association each fall to stage the reorganized State Fair of Texas.

Col. James B. Simpson, an early Dallas attorney and editor of the city's first newspaper, the Dallas *Herald*, served as the first president of the Dallas State Fair and Exposition in 1886. (Courtesy of the State Fair of Texas Archives.)

With the consolidation of two rival fairs held in Dallas in 1886, James Maroney was elected president of the new enterprise that would be known as the Texas State Fair and Dallas Exposition. Fair Park hosted the fair under this new moniker in 1887. Maroney owned a prosperous hardware business in Dallas and was treasurer of the Munger Improved Cotton Manufacturing Company. He was also one of the city's most prominent Irish Catholics, having been elected president of the newly formed local branch of the Irish National League in 1885 and appointed to a committee charged with building a Catholic cathedral in Dallas in 1887. (Courtesy of the State Fair of Texas Archives.)

John S. Armstrong was elected president of the Texas State Fair in 1887. He was a relative newcomer to Dallas, having relocated his wholesale grocery business to the city from Louisville, Kentucky, in 1884. In 1887, following a fire that destroyed not only Armstrong's grocery warehouse but also that of his neighboring competitor, Thomas Marsalis, the two gentlemen announced the consolidation of their grocery businesses into a single enterprise. That same year, Armstrong and Marsalis completed the assembly of almost 2,000 acres of land across the Trinity River from downtown Dallas and began selling lots in a residential development known as Oak Cliff. (Courtesy of the State Fair of Texas Archives.)

Col. Henry Exall was elected the fourth president of the Texas State Fair in 1888. Originally from Lampasas in West Texas, Exall visited Dallas frequently during the early 1880s in his role as chairman of the state Democratic Party executive committee and as a member of the Texas State Bankers Association. He moved to Dallas in 1887 and began to speculate in Dallas real estate. He opened the North Texas National Bank in January 1888 and was among a group of investors that year to charter the Dallas Rapid Transit Company, which provided service between downtown and Fair Park. (Courtesy of the State Fair of Texas Archives.)

In 1886, over 14,000 visitors crowded the fairgrounds on the opening day of the Dallas State Fair and Exposition. This view shows fashionably attired ladies mingling in front of the main entrance to the Exposition Building. An 11-foot-high star adorns the roof of the second-floor gallery. This Lone Star theme would play an important thematic role in the structures built at Fair Park over the next 50 years. (Courtesy of the State Fair of Texas Archives.)

Carriages and wagons accessed the fairgrounds along this street, which bounded Fair Park on its western perimeter. Both temporary exhibits and permanent buildings can be seen in this view of the 1890 Texas State Fair. The second largest exhibit structure on the fairgrounds was Machinery Hall, which is visible in the upper right of this photograph, prominent with its multiple, identical square towers. (Courtesy of the State Fair of Texas Archives.)

Architect James Flanders's massive Exposition Building was one of the largest structures ever built in Dallas when it was completed in 1887. The square towers were a Victorian-era theme that the architect also incorporated into his design of Machinery Hall, giving the two major exhibit buildings at the fairgrounds a consistent appearance. This 1890 photograph was probably taken prior to the pre-fair "load-in" of temporary exhibits and tents that would have packed the vacant field. The road evident in this image stretched from the main entry gate on Parry Avenue to the Exposition Building and served as Fair Park's primary circulation axis until 1936, when it would be transformed into the Esplanade of State for the Texas Centennial Exposition. (Courtesy of the State Fair of Texas Archives.)

Many farm implement manufacturers and dealers, unable to gain space in the 90,000-square-foot Machinery Hall, were often forced to set up outdoor exhibits such as these in an adjacent area known as Machinery Park. Farmers from throughout the state traveled to Dallas each fall to see the latest inventions and developments in farm implements at the state fair. In the above *c.* 1910 image, the tractors exhibited at the state fair by the Hart-Parr Company of Charles City, Iowa, were advertised as "Gasoline Kerosene Distillate Traction Engines." The engine was initially started with gasoline. Then, when it warmed up, the operator changed a valve that switched the fuel source to kerosene. As the engine started to invariably knock, a water valve was opened that provided water injection into the engine to control the combustion knock. In the image below, a farm equipment manufacturer prominently displayed various models of buggies at the *c.* 1900 state fair. (Both, courtesy of the State Fair of Texas Archives.)

This *c.* 1895 view of the fairgrounds shows the large tents and small wooden buildings used by exhibitors to display their products. To the left, the Jos. W. Moon Buggy Company, a manufacturer based in St. Louis, captured fairgoers' attention by stacking wagons to tower over the surroundings. A mule-drawn trolley navigated its way through Fair Park on tracks laid out in the unpaved streets. When it rained, the black, clay soil transformed the fairgrounds into "the worst kind of hog wallow," according to the *Dallas Morning News*. (Courtesy of the Dallas Municipal Archives.)

This 1887 view shows the newly completed Machinery Hall on the western edge of the fairgrounds. The photograph was taken from Parry Avenue, with one of the two horse-drawn trolley lines that served the fairgrounds evident in the foreground. Stretching between Parry Avenue and Machinery Hall was a barren, 14-acre parcel owned by Capt. W. H. Gaston. Gaston Park, as the property came to be known, was used for athletic events during the fair and was eventually sold to the City of Dallas in 1914. The site was utilized for parking throughout the 1920s and was officially incorporated into the fairgrounds in 1925 with the construction of the Fair Park Auditorium. (Courtesy of the Dallas Municipal Archives.)

By 1895, much of the fairgrounds had been transformed into an extravagantly landscaped park with mature trees and luxurious vegetation. This view shows a generous public garden area, slightly lower than the surrounding grade, edged in foliage with large, round planting beds in the center. Machinery Hall can be seen in the background. (Courtesy of the Dallas Municipal Archives.)

The main entry gate to the fairgrounds, located on Parry Avenue, was built for the first fair in 1886. It marked the location of the primary entrance to Fair Park up to the present day. This wooden structure served as the fair's main entrance until its demolition and replacement in 1906 by a grander masonry portal. (Courtesy of the Dallas Municipal Archives.)

In 1904, the Texas State Fair was reorganized and renamed the State Fair of Texas. In this view, officers of the new organization pose in front of the main entry gate on Parry Avenue. They include, from left to right, Cecil Keating, president; Charles Mangold, chairman of the attraction and amusement committee; Edwin Kiest, director; and Capt. Sydney Smith, longtime secretary of the fair. (Courtesy of the State Fair of Texas Archives.)

Horse racing played a prominent role in the early state fairs. It was the fair's primary attraction and served as its principal source of revenue. Both of these *c.* 1900 images show the generous appointments accorded the racetrack. In the above view, two separate grandstands are visible, the larger seating 8,000. To the right of the main grandstand in this view is Machinery Hall with its distinctive square towers, and farther to the right is the fair's main Exposition Building. In the below image, privileged fairgoers were accorded a separate and more exclusive seating area so as not to mix with the common racing throngs. The octagonal judges' stand was a distinctive element in the infield of the racetrack. Above the far fence of the track are the cotton fields east of Dallas, extending to the horizon. (Above, courtesy of the Texas/Dallas History and Archives Division, Dallas Public Library; below, courtesy of the Dallas Historical Society Archives.)

SCENE ON RACE TRACK — TEXAS STATE FAIR GROUNDS.

Harness races were also staged at the horse track during the run of the Texas State Fair. Prior to the 1903 event, the Texas legislature banned betting on horse races. Revenues that year dropped by almost 50 percent, which was the final straw in a series of events that threw the fair into financial calamity. Two years earlier, James Flanders's Exposition Building, prominent in this view, burned to the ground in a spectacular conflagration that could be seen 35 miles away. Unable to afford a replacement exhibit building and now without racing revenues to bolster its fragile finances, the fair association was forced to negotiate a deal with the City of Dallas in 1904. In exchange for $125,000 in cash that would retire debt and go toward the construction of a new exhibit hall, the fairgrounds were deeded to the city and became Dallas's second public park, known as Fair Park. The reorganized fair was renamed the State Fair of Texas. (Courtesy of the Dallas Historical Society Archives.)

Advertising posters such as this 1890 broadside highlighting horse racing were published each year by the Texas State Fair and distributed throughout the state. (Courtesy of the Dallas Historical Society Archives.)

In 1904, the Texas State Fair was reorganized and the grounds dedicated to the city. Several years later, the State Fair of Texas board hired prominent Kansas City landscape architect George Kessler to produce the first master plan for the fairgrounds, now known as Fair Park. He enhanced the existing plan of the park by arranging drives and promenades and by specifying the locations of future structures. The first of these to be constructed was a new exhibit building and auditorium to replace the previous one that burned in 1902. Dallas architect James Flanders, who designed the earlier structure, once again was enlisted to design the replacement facility, which was completed in 1905. He proposed a 75,000-square-foot, fire-proof building with a steel structure clad in stone. It is interesting to note that while Flanders was elected to the Dallas City Council as an alderman in April 1904, there was apparently no conflict of interest in the multiple commissions for projects he received at the city-owned Fair Park. (Both, courtesy of the State Fair of Texas Archives.)

OPPOSITE: This 1908 panoramic view shows the dramatic improvement of the Parry Avenue entrance to Fair Park after the original wooden entry gate to the fairgrounds was replaced by a new masonry pedestrian gate in 1906. Temporary ticket booths set up to handle the massive crowds for the state fair can be seen in front of this gate. A new vehicular gate, to the right of the pedestrian gate designed by James Flanders, was completed in 1908. Visible above the main gate is the prominent dome of the Textile and Fine Arts Building. In the distance to the right are the three gabled bays of the 1905 Exposition Hall. (Courtesy of the Library of Congress.)

TWO

THE GREAT STATE FAIR

With the burden of debts removed by the influx of cash from the city, the State Fair Association could focus on replacing and expanding old facilities and improving the grounds at Fair Park. The renowned landscape architect and planner from Kansas City, George Kessler, was hired to replan and landscape the fairgrounds and to identify sites for future buildings. His scheme was a manifestation of the City Beautiful movement and his own recent planning experience at the 1904 world's fair in St. Louis. He proposed a broad, pedestrian promenade interspersed with plazas and fountains that extended from the entrance of the fairgrounds on Parry Avenue to the racetrack. The significance of this plan was that it would be strictly adhered to over the following three decades as new buildings were added at Fair Park. Kessler's plan, which was completed in 1906, formed the basis of the layout for the Texas Centennial Exposition in 1936.

Beginning in 1905, major new projects were completed at the fairgrounds in rapid succession—a reflection of renewed confidence and investment by the State Fair Association and of Fair Park's importance to Dallas. This construction campaign continued unabated until 1930, by which time a new automobile and manufacturers hall and a music hall had been completed and a new football stadium was under construction. The existing buildings and venues at Fair Park formed the framework for the layout of the Texas Centennial Exposition in 1936 and would be integrated into its final plan.

Several state fair directors, including Charles Mangold (second from left), Cecil Keating (third from left), and Capt. Sydney Smith (third from right) pose for a photograph in 1904 at the concrete foundation wall of the new Exposition Hall. (Courtesy of the State Fair of Texas Archives.)

Exposition Hall opened on October 28, 1905, with a dedication ceremony in the building's 3,500-seat auditorium. Luminaries seated on the dais in the front row included state fair president Cecil Keating, Gov. S. W. T. Lanham, Sen. Charles Culberson, Mayor Bryan T. Barry, and Episcopal bishop A. C. Garrett. Performers and groups booked for the auditorium during the state fair that year included the Olympia Opera Company and soloist Eugenia Munzesheimer. (Courtesy of the State Fair of Texas Archives.)

In 1907, a flat-roofed addition, which contained agricultural and manufacturing displays, was completed across the rear side of Exposition Hall. This part of the building would be demolished in 1936 as the entire structure was adapted and modified to fit in with the new layout and architectural theme of the Texas Centennial Exposition. (Courtesy of the State Fair of Texas Archives.)

Children and young ladies pose in front of Exposition Hall in this *c.* 1925 view. The landscaping adjacent to the entrances to the exhibit hall has grown more prominent since the building's completion in 1905. (Author's collection.)

In 1905, the amusement and restaurant zone of the fairgrounds was renamed "The Pike," in tribute to the amusement area of the same name at the 1904 Louisiana Purchase Exposition in St. Louis. In this 1905 image (above) is the Bohemian Garden, the three-story structure on the right, beyond which Restaurant Row is visible through the trees. Restaurant Row (below) was constructed in 1896 but was more popularly known to fairgoers as "Old Smoky," in reference to the sometimes dense smoke and miasma produced by charitable groups cooking food for hungry state fair patrons. (Both, courtesy of the State Fair of Texas Archives.)

The Louisiana Purchase Exposition of 1904 in St. Louis was the greatest fair held in the United States since the World's Columbian Exposition had been staged in Chicago in 1893 and 1894. State fair fathers traveled to the St. Louis fair and brought back to Texas many exhibits and attractions for the 1905 event in Dallas. Weighing from one to six tons each, 26 plaster statues were salvaged from the Belgian Building at the fair in St. Louis and shipped back to Dallas on three rail flat cars for installation at the fairgrounds. Monumental sculptures were installed on top of the recently completed bandstand and on a masonry arch that served the fairgrounds as a post office. One visitor to the fairgrounds declared that the statuary placed on the buildings imparted "a classical air to the park." (Above, courtesy of the State Fair of Texas Archives; below, courtesy of thee Texas/Dallas History and Archives Division, Dallas Public Library.)

VIEW IN FAIR PARK.

Completed in 1908 at a cost of $47,000, the Textile and Fine Arts Building provided Dallas with its first permanent art museum. Designed by the Dallas architectural firm Hubbell and Greene, it was one of the earliest examples in the city of the grand classical style popularized as the "White City" at Chicago's Columbian Exposition of 1893. It was located next to the Exposition Building, facing George Kessler's landscaped promenade, which extended from behind the main entry gate on Parry Avenue. Square in plan, the Textile and Fine Arts Building was surmounted by a large dome with glass skylights and featured a smaller dome at each of the four corners. This picturesque arrangement closely followed the design of the magnificent Horticultural Hall at the Chicago exposition. (Courtesy of the State Fair of Texas Archives.)

The broad, grassy lawn and pedestrian promenade proposed by George Kessler in his 1906 master plan for Fair Park is evident in the above image. To the left in this view is the Exposition Hall, completed in 1905, and to the right is a replica of the Alamo. This notable feature was donated by the *Dallas Morning News* to Fair Park with the intent of augmenting "in the minds of the younger generation . . . that proper patriotic feeling and pride for the small but noble band which fought and died for the freedom which we now enjoy." The original mission chapel in San Antonio was carefully measured by the architects, Hubbell and Greene, and a replica was constructed at a reduced scale in the two months leading up to the 1909 state fair. In the image below, three well-dressed men relax on the promenade following a rare Dallas snowstorm. (Both, courtesy of the State Fair of Texas Archives.)

In August 1909, a military tournament was held in the infield of the racetrack at Fair Park. Over 2,000 troops from Fort Sam Houston in San Antonio participated, including the U.S. Army Ninth Infantry, the Third Cavalry, and the First Field Artillery. The tournament featured competitive precision marching, horseback drills, artillery demonstrations, equipment contests, and band performances on Sunday. During their week at Fair Park, the troops were estimated to consume over 11,000 pounds of beef, 12,320 pounds of flour, 8,800 pounds of potatoes, and 1,100 pounds of coffee. The horses were equally hungry, consuming over 50,000 pounds of hay and 40,000 pounds of oats. (Courtesy of the State Fair of Texas Archives.)

Pres. William Howard Taft was the first American president to visit Fair Park, during the 1909 state fair. Taft passed through Dallas near the end of a 12,000-mile-long goodwill tour to the West Coast. The president's train, which arrived from Houston at 5:30 p.m., was switched from the Houston and Texas Central Railroad main line to a secondary track and siding that took it to the front of the state fair administration building on Parry Avenue. From there, Taft was conveyed to the racetrack grandstand where he delivered a speech to 8,000 enthusiastic spectators. His short route through Fair Park was witnessed by an estimated 100,000 people. This photograph was taken as the president passed by the arched openings of the administration building, seen in the right background. (Courtesy of the State Fair of Texas Archives.)

Architect H. A. Overbeck employed the Mission Revival style for this handsome new state fair administration building, which was completed in 1906 at a cost of $15,000. Stylistically, it was an odd choice for Fair Park, given the more classically inspired buildings that preceded it. After the completion of Exposition Hall the previous year, state fair directors desired to bring the exterior of the park into harmony with the interior. The building also served as the main pedestrian gateway to Fair Park, allowing people alighting from the streetcars on Parry Avenue to pass through turnstiles under cover and enabling visitors to traverse the grounds without wading through mud. (Courtesy of the Texas/Dallas History and Archives Division, Dallas Public Library.)

Dallas's first Coliseum was constructed by the state fair in 1910, primarily for horse shows, but it was also utilized for musical entertainment throughout the year. Its location along the front boundary of Fair Park, immediately inside the entry gate, allowed access from inside the park during fair time, as well as direct access from Parry Avenue. The architect was C. D. Hill, who would design Dallas's grand Municipal Building in downtown three years later. In 1935, this building would be renovated as the Texas Centennial Exposition's administrative offices. (Both, courtesy of the Texas/Dallas History and Archives Division, Dallas Public Library.)

These *c.* 1912 interior views of the Coliseum illustrate the building's programmatic flexibility, with its ability to host both horse shows and Grand Opera—on the same dirt floor. In 1911, New Jersey governor Woodrow Wilson delivered an address to 6,000 in the Coliseum in a test of his presidential candidacy. In 1912, the newly organized Dallas Symphony Orchestra played a series of concerts in the structure. Sometime after 1915, a sloping wood floor with permanent seats was installed. (Above, courtesy of the Dallas Municipal Archives; below, courtesy of the State Fair of Texas Archives.)

The Coliseum was the third and final building in an impressive array of public facilities built on the north side of George Kessler's promenade at Fair Park. Over a five-year period, the City of Dallas and the State Fair Association, working together in partnership, funded a major exhibition hall, a Textile and Fine Arts Building (at right in this view), and a coliseum seating 8,000. (Courtesy of the Dallas Municipal Archives.)

The Coliseum (left) and the state fair entry gate (right) presented a monumental urban facade to the city along Parry Avenue. Tracks of the Dallas Rapid Transit Company can be seen in the still unpaved street in this *c.* 1911 view. (Courtesy of the Dallas Municipal Archives.)

Following the tremendous success of the amusement area known as "The Pike" in St. Louis in 1904, the State Fair of Texas directors determined that a similar scheme in Dallas could be highly profitable. Starting in 1906, new rides were installed at Fair Park, including the 1,125-foot-long Scenic Railway (seen in the background of both images) and a water slide called Shoot the Chute (above on the right and below). In 1908, another spectacular attraction was added: a second roller coaster called The Tickler. (Above, courtesy of the Texas/Dallas History and Archives Division, Dallas Public Library; below, courtesy of the State Fair of Texas Archives.)

In 1912, the state fair razed the decrepit Restaurant Row food pavilion called Old Smoky and replaced it with a new, modern Restaurant and Cafe Building at a cost of $35,000. This enormous structure was 700 feet in length and included a two-story cafe at its midpoint with an elegantly furnished dining hall on the second floor, where the menu was purported to be the equal of any first-class hotel. (Both, courtesy of the State Fair of Texas Archives.)

Horse races returned to Fair Park in 1905 when the state legislature exempted on-site wagering from the 1903 ban on betting. In 1909, however, the state reversed this action and once again outlawed wagering on horse races in Texas. State fair directors were desperate to create revenue and began to schedule alternative events and attractions in the racetrack to draw admission-paying crowds. Aviation shows were huge attractions that often filled the racetrack grandstands. In 1911, the state fair booked the McCurdy-Willard Aeroplane Company of New York for aerial performances each afternoon (above and opposite page). When pilot J. A. D. McCurdy wrecked his flying machine in a high wind, aviator Cal Rodgers, who was making a cross-country flight through North Texas in a Wright machine at the time, was induced to make a stopover at the fairgrounds. (Courtesy of the Dallas Historical Society Archives.)

Adjustments are made to a flying machine in the racetrack infield while spectators in the distance watch. (Courtesy of the Texas/Dallas History and Archives Division, Dallas Public Library.)

Capacity crowds were also on hand at the track for auto racing. At the 1920 state fair, one Saturday racing program consisted of seven events of varying lengths up to 10 miles, culminating at the end of the day with the 15-mile-long Southwestern Derby. Between $10,000 and $20,000 was typically offered as prize money over the duration of the state fair. In this 1920 image, cars are escorted to the starting line. Manufacturers of the automobiles that raced at the State Fair of Texas included Dusenberg, Essex, Stutz, Oldfield, Fiat, Bugatti, and Frontenac. (Courtesy of the State Fair of Texas Archives.)

In 1913, the state fair constructed a permanent exhibit building for automobiles. It was a shrewd investment with a minimal cost and provided the fairgrounds with an enormously popular new attraction. Located beyond the racetrack grandstands at the far edge of Fair Park, the wooden structure could accommodate the display of 225 cars and trucks. The 1913 show was the first of its type ever held in Texas, drawing the attention of Detroit automotive executives who traveled to Dallas on two special Pullman cars to see the event. (Courtesy of the State Fair of Texas Archives.)

Between 1911 and 1913, the state fair invested over $80,000 in new livestock facilities. Over the previous decade, barns and show arenas had been consolidated on the north side of the racetrack adjacent to the railroad spur for easy loading of livestock. By 1910, the state fair was staging the largest livestock show in the nation, but the facilities were inadequate to accommodate further growth. In this image, the new livestock barns (right), completed in 1913, provided space for 500 head of cattle and pens for 500 sheep and 1,500 hogs. The building was of fireproof, concrete construction with roof monitor windows that allowed in natural light. Various three-dimensional animal heads projected from the front wall. The two-story section at the far left of this view covered the front of the Livestock Pavilion, which was built in 1911. (Courtesy of the Dallas Park and Recreation Department.)

Large, well-dressed crowds were a common sight at the state fair. In the 1916 photograph (above), fairgoers rest on George Kessler's landscaped promenade. The 1921 image (below) shows people strolling between the amusement area known as "The Pike" on the left and the racetrack grandstands on the right. (Both, courtesy of the State Fair of Texas Archives.)

This *c.* 1922 aerial image of the eastern section of Fair Park shows the 15,000-seat football stadium, which was completed in 1921. To the left of the stadium is the Automobile Building. (Author's collection.)

Fair Park Stadium was the site of three major college football games in October during the 1921 state fair. In the first game, A&M College (now Texas A&M) defeated Southern Methodist University 13-0. This was the Aggies' 18th shutout victory in their last 19 football games. The next weekend, Boston College beat Baylor 23-7 in the first game ever played between teams from the southwest and the northeast. On the final weekend of the fair, the University of Texas lost to Vanderbilt 20-0. Both teams came into this game undefeated. In the image below, the Texas Longhorn marching band takes the field during halftime of the game with the Vanderbilt Commodores. (Both, courtesy of the State Fair of Texas Archives.)

Two aerial views of Fair Park (this page and opposite) illustrate the impressive layout of the state fair and the magnificent facilities that had been constructed on the fairgrounds since 1905. (Courtesy of the Dallas Municipal Archives.)

In this 1924 view, the Automobile and Manufacturers Building can be seen to the lower right of the racetrack. On the east side of the track (upper left) is the livestock complex for the fairgrounds, including the Livestock Pavilion and barns. The state fair administration building is visible along Parry Avenue at the bottom of this image. George Kessler's pedestrian promenade stretches between it and the track, with the Coliseum, Textile and Fine Arts Building, and Exposition Hall arrayed along this axis to the left. (Author's collection.)

By the early 1920s, the original Automobile Building was viewed as an embarrassment by the state fair and had grown wholly inadequate to satisfy the space demands of the North Texas car dealers. The fair association worked with automobile retailers and manufacturers to finance a major new exhibit building, which was completed in 1922. Built near the site of the fairgrounds' original Manufacturers Hall, the Mission Revival–style Automobile and Manufacturers Building was 500 feet in length and featured twin towers at each end with a distinctive "Alamo" parapet profile on the gables. (Courtesy of the State Fair of Texas Archives.)

The Automobile and Manufacturers Building was divided between auto exhibits (in the *c.* 1928 image above), which had 300 linear feet of space, and manufacturing exhibits (in the *c.* 1925 image below), which were allotted 200 linear feet. The Dr. Pepper soda fountain was a popular attraction in the manufacturers' end of the exhibit hall. (Both, courtesy of the State Fair of Texas Archives.)

The $500,000 Fair Park Auditorium was completed in 1925 on the old Gaston Park tract adjacent to Parry Avenue. The cavernous 3,500-seat music hall, designed by Lang and Witchell, incorporated Spanish Colonial Revival detailing, primarily in the dominant square towers on the building's north side and in the paired octagonal towers on the east and west facades. The building continued the Spanish architectural theme established by the nearby Automobile and Manufacturers Building, which had similar twin towers. The auditorium was one of the grandest concert halls in America. *The Student Prince* was booked as the first show during the 1925 state fair. (Courtesy of the Dallas Historical Society Archives.)

This 1929 photograph shows the state fair administration building (left) and, beyond it, the twin pylons that marked the 1908 vehicular entry gate to Fair Park. These structures would be demolished in 1935 to build the grand entry gate for the Texas Centennial Exposition. (Courtesy of the State Fair of Texas Archives.)

These two images of the state fair midway, from 1924 and *c.* 1925, illustrate the sometimes seedy character of the amusement attractions and concessions found in this area of the fairgrounds. All of the structures and most of the rides would be demolished to make room for the new midway at the Texas Centennial Exposition. (Both, courtesy of the State Fair of Texas Archives.)

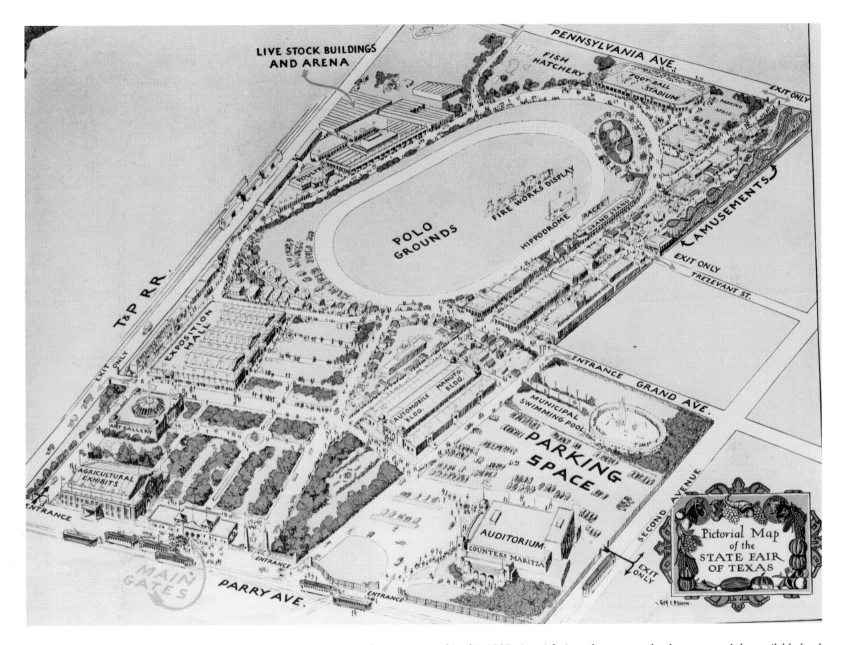

Fair Park, as it appeared in this 1927 pictorial view, almost completely consumed the available land of the fairgrounds, with the exception of the infield of the old racetrack. The track, which dated back to the very first fair in 1886, would finally be removed in 1930 to provide space for a new football stadium. (Courtesy of the Dallas Municipal Archives.)

The tremendous success of the 15,000-seat football stadium built in 1921 prompted the City of Dallas and the State Fair Association to make plans for a new, larger stadium. Architect Mark Lemmon designed a bowl, partially recessed in the ground, with a 46-foot-high landscaped embankment that completely encircled the field. The seating capacity was 46,200, making it the largest stadium in the South. Construction began in May 1930, with the official groundbreaking taking place in the center of the racetrack infield. Present for this ceremony are, from left to right, Roy Rupard, state fair secretary; Foster Jacoby, parks director; Laura Yeary Smith, the first female member of the park board; Edgar Hurst, park board vice president; Dallas mayor Waddy Tate; Phil Prather, State Fair Stadium Committee chairman; structural engineer Carl Forrest; contractor Gifford Hill; and architect Mark Lemmon. The grandstand of the racetrack can be seen in the distance. (Courtesy of the State Fair of Texas Archives.)

The new Fair Park Stadium is prominent in this 1930 postcard view of the park, in which the outline of the old racetrack can be seen encircling the stadium. The 60 acres of land between the stadium embankment and the edge of the former track were used for parking. Fair Park Auditorium can be seen in the lower right. In 1936, prior to the Texas Centennial Exposition, the stadium was renamed the Cotton Bowl. (Author's collection.)

Texas Centennial Exposition architect George Dahl was a relative newcomer to Dallas, having arrived in the city in 1926 to work in the office of the distinguished architect Herbert M. Greene. The talented young draftsman was promoted to partner in 1928 and quickly assimilated into the upper echelon of Dallas's business fraternity, where he met the powerful banker R. L. Thornton. The two men worked tirelessly side-by-side to assist in the campaign to lure the proposed Texas Centennial Exposition to Dallas. Dahl was rewarded for his extraordinary efforts with a contract as the official Texas Centennial Exposition architect. (Courtesy of Adrienne Faulkner, Faulkner Design Group and Architectural-Images.com.)

OPPOSITE: Dahl's initial task as architect was the assembly of a competent technical and design staff made up of architects, engineers, and artists: a multi-disciplined team of over 130 people, unprecedented in 1935 for its collaborative nature and size. Critical members of Dahl's staff had previous experience at two other American expositions during the 1930s. In this view of the design and construction staff, taken inside the Hall of Administration in 1935, George Dahl is on the far right, cigar in hand. Donald Nelson, Dahl's chief architect and veteran of the Chicago Century of Progress Exposition, is in the second row, third from the left. (Courtesy of the Dallas Historical Society Archives.)

THREE

FROM STATE FAIR TO WORLD'S FAIR

Plans for a statewide centennial celebration were formulated by the state Centennial Commission in 1934, at which time a central exposition was formally proposed. The commission publicized the scope and historical nature of the exposition and the requirements for any city wishing to bid for it. The campaign to secure Dallas's designation as the host city for this auspicious event was skillfully orchestrated by banker R. L. Thornton with energetic assistance provided by architect George Dahl. Dahl, who had previously traveled to six expositions in the United States and Europe, worked tirelessly alongside Thornton to bring the Texas Centennial Exposition to his adopted home. Dahl's office produced a series of seven conjectural renderings ("eyewash" in his own words) that Thornton used—along with a bid of $7,791,000—to persuade members of the Centennial Commission. In late 1934, Dallas was selected to host the Texas Centennial Exposition.

The city's total investment in the exposition would ultimately rise to over $25 million, making it the second costliest world's fair ever held in America up to that time. Soon after the selection was announced, Dahl was rewarded for his efforts with a contract as Texas Centennial Exposition architect. Commensurate with this long sought-after position was the daunting task of planning, designing, and constructing the Texas Centennial Exposition in a little over 14 months.

The equally grandiose scheme for the State of Texas Building is pictured above. These renderings had the desired effect: Dallas was selected to host the exposition. (Courtesy of Adrienne Faulkner, Faulkner Design Group and Architectural-Images.com.)

To help lure the exposition to Dallas, Dahl's firm created a series of speculative representations ("eyewash" in his own words) that R. L. Thornton used to win over members of the state Centennial Commission. The image above illustrates Dahl's early vision for a monumental entrance plaza, flanked by towering pylons. (Courtesy of Adrienne Faulkner, Faulkner Design Group and Architectural-Images.com.)

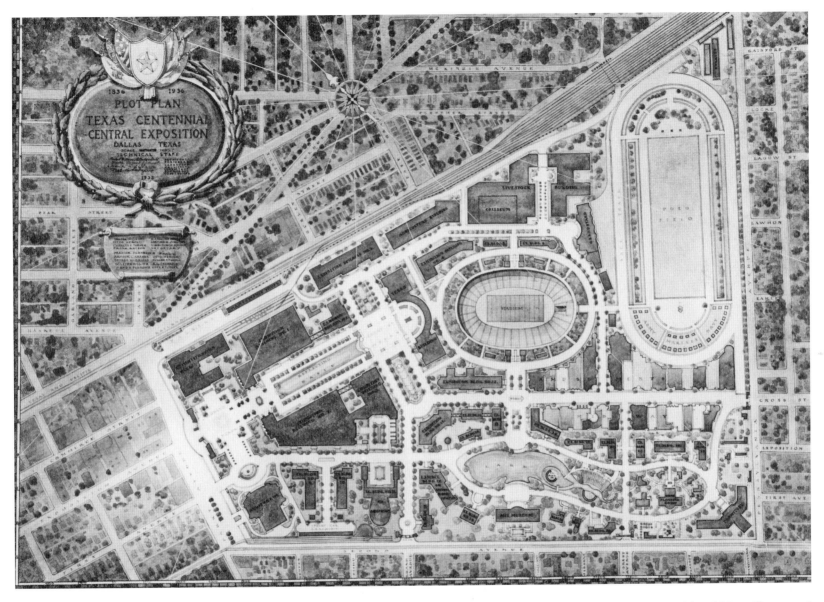

The preliminary site plan for the exposition developed by George Dahl and his staff possessed many of the salient features that would ultimately be incorporated into the final plan at Fair Park. Road realignments and circulation axes have all been firmly established in this plan, as have the proximate locations of all the major new buildings. Dahl strengthened the pedestrian promenade that led from the Parry Avenue entrance to the proposed State of Texas Building (to the left of Fair Park Stadium) by reconfiguring and expanding the two existing exhibition halls on either side of the axis. A lagoon was added in a new section of the fairgrounds (below the stadium), around which was grouped new museums that were proposed for the exposition. (Courtesy of the Dallas Historical Society Archives.)

This is perhaps the final photograph, taken in 1935, of the Coliseum (left) and the state fair administration building (right) prior to their reconfiguration or demolition for the Texas Centennial Exposition. The Coliseum, built in 1910, would be stripped of its porticoes and decorative moldings and be given a modern makeover as the Hall of Administration for the exposition. The old administration building, constructed in 1906, would be demolished and replaced by a new, grand entrance to the fair. (Courtesy of the State Fair of Texas Archives.)

The bronze Gulf Clouds Fountain, by Dallas artist Clyde Gitner Chandler, was dedicated in 1916 in its original location inside the main gate to the fairgrounds. For the Texas Centennial Exposition, it was transported to a new plaza in front of the 1925 auditorium.

Excavation of the foundation of the Swine Building is under way in May 1935. Existing Fair Park structures evident in this image include the grandstand for a horse track (left), built in 1934 after betting was legalized once again by the Texas legislature. The new track had been built in the northeast corner of the fairgrounds. The grandstand would be incorporated as seating for the *Cavalcade of Texas*, an extravagant outdoor performance spectacle during the Texas Centennial Exposition. To the right is the 1913 livestock barn, which would soon receive an art deco face-lift for the exposition. The high-mast light towers seen beyond the livestock barn mark the location of Fair Park Stadium. The perimeter berm of the stadium can be seen in the distance, beyond the excavations. (Courtesy of the State Fair of Texas Archives.)

Thos. Bate & Son.
1706 Cockrell St.
Contractor.

Construction at Fair Park progresses in early 1936, six months prior to the opening of the Texas Centennial Exposition. Noticeable in this aerial view is the Esplanade of State (center left), a 700-foot-long reflecting basin that is flanked by six tall portico structures. These porticoes have been added to the fronts of the old Exposition Hall (1905), located to the left of the esplanade, and the Automobile and Manufacturers Building (1922), located to the right. George Dahl skillfully adapted these two existing structures into the new layout of the fairgrounds. At the head of the esplanade, located just below the stadium, is the steel structure of the State of Texas Building, which would become the centerpiece of the exposition. (Courtesy of the Dallas Historical Society Archives.)

The State of Texas Building was not completed until September 1936, three months after the exposition opened. In this view, stone cladding nears completion on the building's two side wings, but the central, semicircular exedra is still a steel frame. (Courtesy of the Dallas Historical Society Archives.)

Photographs of smiling young ladies with cowboy hats posing on various Fair Park building sites were taken to generate publicity of Texas hospitality for the Texas Centennial Exposition. (Author's collection.)

FEDERAL BLDG.
J.J. FRITCH-GEN'L CONTRACTOR
5-6-36

In the above image, plaster panels are added to the tower of the U.S. Government Building in early 1936. Fireproof clay blocks, the primary building material for many of the new centennial structures, are stacked in the foreground. The bas-relief panels located at the base of the federal building, in the image below, were the work of the sculptor Julian Garnsey. This impressive art piece depicted the history of Texas from 1540—the date of the first Spanish exploration—to 1936. (Above, courtesy of the Dallas Historical Society Archives; below, courtesy of the Texas/Dallas History and Archives Division, Dallas Public Library.)

In the spring of 1936, major exhibit buildings, museums, and livestock facilities neared completion at Fair Park in the months leading up to the Texas Centennial Exposition. In the above image, limestone panels are lifted into place on the Museum of Natural History. Below, buildings in the agriculture and livestock area are nearing completion; only paving work remains. (Both, courtesy of the State Fair of Texas Archives.)

The National Cash Register exhibit nears completion in the image at left. In the image below, only finishing touches remain at the fairgrounds in the month prior to the Texas Centennial Exposition. The rear of the Ford Motor Company Building can be seen at the far left of this view, and the National Cash Register exhibit is in the far distance above the treetops and surrounding structures. On the far shore of the lagoon, the Forbidden City still has scaffolding. The Museum of Natural History is on the right. (Above, courtesy of the State Fair of Texas Archives; below, courtesy of the Dallas Historical Society Archives.)

Final landscaping occurs in the Rio Grande Valley exhibit, which was located on a leftover tract of land situated between several exhibit buildings. The rear of three different structures can be seen in this image. They are, from near top left to right, the Gulf Oil exhibit, the Skillern's Drugstore exhibit, and the Texas Flour Milling Industry exhibit. (Courtesy of the Dallas Historical Society Archives.)

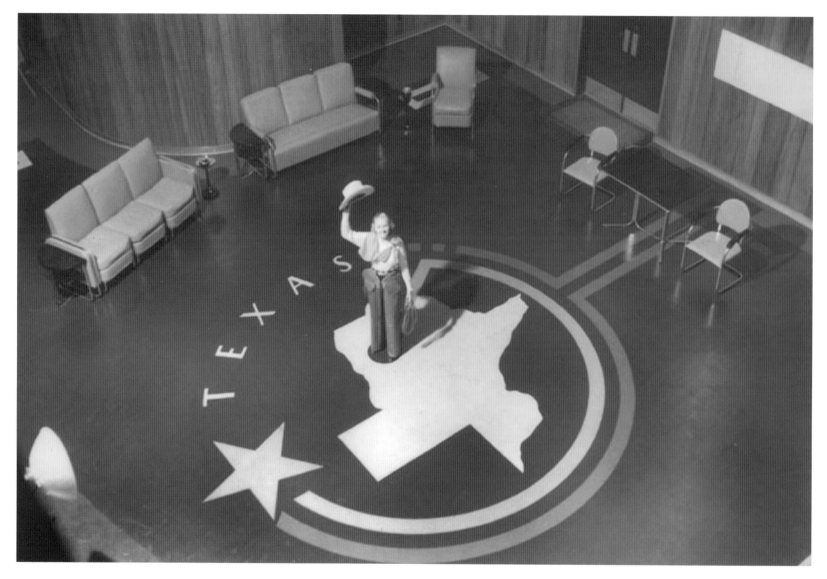

In this publicity photograph, a cowgirl issues a big Texas welcome to Dallas and the Texas Centennial Exposition. The photograph was taken in the lobby of the Hall of Administration, which served as the Texas Centennial Exposition's headquarters before and during the fair. Prior to its renovation into office space, the building had served Fair Park as a livestock coliseum. The modern furnishings seen in this view were probably designed by Gilbert Rohde for Herman Miller. (Courtesy of the Dallas Historical Society Archives.)

OPPOSITE: This grand vista of the Esplanade of State and the State of Texas Building greeted visitors who entered the fairgrounds at Parry Avenue. It was a majestic spectacle carefully choreographed by the Texas Centennial Exposition architect, George Dahl. (Courtesy of the Texas/Dallas History and Archives Division, Dallas Public Library.)

THE YEAR AMERICA DISCOVERED DALLAS

Opening to the public on June 6, 1936, the Texas Centennial Exposition was not only a celebration of Texas independence, but also a festival of architecture, art, and light. It was the first air-conditioned world's fair—a necessity demanded by the Dallas climate and made achievable through recent advances in building technology. Designed by George Dahl and his talented team of architect-artist collaborators in the moderne style, the geometric crispness and bold color of the new and remodeled buildings stood out in sharp contrast under the bright Texas sun. Dahl described the theme of the exposition as "Texanic" and "Southwestern," exemplifying in his words "the color, romance and grandeur that had marked the development of Texas . . . the romance of Spain and Mexico, combined with the culture of the Old South."

Activities during the six-month-long fair were predictably varied. The Empire on Parade had over 130 exhibitors and concessionaires, representing every major industry in the United States. Rapid advances in the fields of science and industry formed the predominant theme. While the scientific exhibits amazed as much as they informed, the social and cultural experiences had an even greater lasting impact on exposition visitors, who enjoyed multiple opportunities to savor fine art, music, drama, and folk culture. Celebrities were in abundance: movie stars, radio personalities, national and state politicians, and other famous people whose names brought immediate identity and excitement to the cross section of society that came to the fair. And finally, there was the midway, where the exhibits were both entertaining and informative, and sometimes scandalous.

Advertising posters such as these heralding both the statewide centennial celebration and the exposition were created by the Centennial Commission for distribution to tourist agencies throughout the nation. Over one million visitors from outside of Texas were estimated to have attended the exposition in Dallas. (Both, courtesy of the Dallas Municipal Archives.)

This aerial view of the exposition illustrates the deft and seamless merger of existing structures constructed at Fair Park—the oldest dating back to 1905—with the new buildings and attractions created for the Texas Centennial Exposition. In the lower left corner of this image is the Coliseum, built in 1910 and remodeled in 1935 to serve as the exposition's administrative offices. Above it, the structure with the dome was built in 1908 as the Textile and Fine Arts Building. It was converted to a service and maintenance facility during the Texas Centennial Exposition. Above this building, the three gabled bays of James Flanders's 1905 Exposition Hall have been incorporated into a newer, larger exhibit hall. (Courtesy of the Dallas Municipal Archives.)

June 6 was the opening day of the Texas Centennial Exposition. After years of hard work and growing anticipation, the Empire on Parade trekked slowly through downtown Dallas toward the exposition site at Fair Park. Over 250,000 delirious spectators—the largest crowd gathered in the Southwest to that date—witnessed the 3-mile-long spectacle. Newsreel companies and radio stations recorded the events and provided live, in-depth coverage. The official opening ceremony, held at the main gate on Parry Avenue, was broadcast nationally over the major networks. First-day attendance at the exposition was over 117,000. (Courtesy of the State Fair of Texas Archives.)

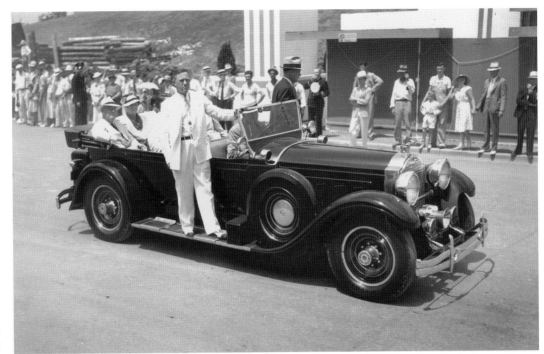

One week later, Pres. Franklin Delano Roosevelt came to Dallas on a pre-reelection campaign swing through Texas. He was greeted by another festive parade through downtown, this one attracting an epic crowd of over 500,000 spectators along the same route as the opening-day parade the week before. In the above view, the president and first lady tour the exposition grounds before entering the Cotton Bowl stadium in a long caravan of automobiles to the delight of the capacity crowd. There President Roosevelt delivered a nationally broadcast address in which he paid tribute to Texas on the occasion of its 100th anniversary and encouraged the nation to visit the exposition. Comprising the world's largest choir, 50,000 Texas schoolchildren performed a program of Texas songs for the national radio audience. (Both, courtesy of the State Fair of Texas Archives.)

Prominent in the lower left of this aerial view of Fair Park is the old 1910 Coliseum, which was remodeled to serve as the exposition's Hall of Administration. To the right is the new entrance to the fair on Parry Avenue. Stretching behind this gate are the Grand Plaza and Esplanade of State, with its 700-foot-long reflecting pool and fountains. The terminus of the esplanade and the architectural centerpiece of the entire exposition was the State of Texas Building. (Courtesy of the Dallas Municipal Archives.)

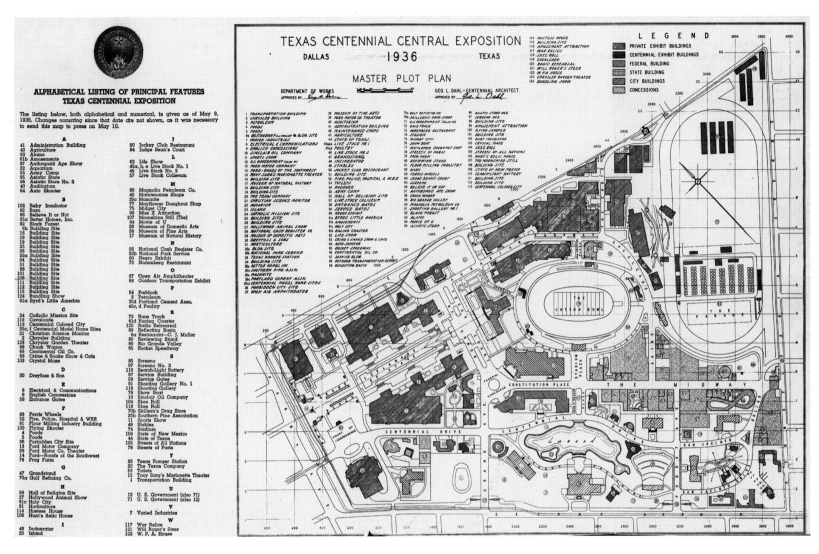

This official site plan of the Texas Centennial Exposition illustrates the system of streets and pedestrian concourses at Fair Park as well as the placement and arrangement of buildings. Of equal interest are the more subtle elements of this plan, including axes and alignments utilized by Dahl and his staff to create visual focal points throughout the fairgrounds, and the hierarchy and relationship of buildings and the spaces between them, which created a comfortable and meaningful public realm for the fair's visitors. (Author's collection.)

The main entrance gate to the exposition established the "six flags" theme that permeated the fairgrounds. To the left and right of the main plaza, flags depicting the six nations that ruled Texas— from left to right, France, the Confederacy, the United States, the Republic of Texas, Mexico, and Spain—are part of an intricate, hierarchical composition that included a tower, cubic buildings, light pylons with engaged flagpoles, and small pavilions. The entire scene was dramatically lit at night. In the distance is Fair Park Auditorium, which was adapted as an exhibit hall for General Motors. (Courtesy of the Dallas Municipal Archives.)

Over 6.5 million visitors to the Texas Centennial Exposition passed through the Parry Avenue entrance gate over the six-month course of the fair. Opening day, seen in this image, was particularly hectic. Dominating over the plaza was a 100-foot-tall tower with a three-dimensional Lone Star at the top that was back-lit at night. At its base, visitors passed through two parallel rows of pavilions—the first for ticketing, the second for turnstiles. The image below is a ticket stub to the exposition. (Above, courtesy of the Texas/Dallas History and Archives Division, Dallas Public Library; below, author's collection.)

56.—Esplanade and State Bldg.   Texas Centennial Exposition
OFFICIAL PHOTO — SI RIGO.

George Dahl framed the view looking down the esplanade toward the State of Texas Building with new exhibit buildings on each side of the 700-foot-long fountain. Each of these buildings incorporated an existing state fair exhibit hall into its new floor plan. On the left of these images, the 1905 Exposition Hall received a new moderne facade to become the fair's Hall of Transportation and was extended with a new wing that served as the Chrysler Motors Building. On the right, the 1922 Automobile and Manufacturers Building was transformed with a sizable addition into the Hall of Electricity and Communications and the Hall of Varied Industries. Murals on the exterior of each building portrayed the theme of the exhibits contained within. The postcard image of the esplanade shows two decorative pylons designed by the artist Pierre Bourdelle. (Both, author's collection.)

The exhibit halls on each side of the esplanade had three projecting portico entries featuring a recessed area topped by a rounded arch called an *entrado*. A 20-foot-tall monumental sculpture representing one of the six nations that ruled Texas was set within each of these arched alcoves. In front of the *entrados* were a set of four oversized, billowing flags that represented the same country as the sculpture. In this view, flags of the United States, Mexico, and France can be seen on the south side of the esplanade in front of the Hall of Electricity and Communications and the Hall of Varied Industries. The effect of the esplanade, with its underlying theme of Texas history, must have been awe-inspiring to the fair's small-town visitors who had never before encountered modernistic architecture. (Author's collection.)

The arrangement of porticoes, *entrados*, sculpture, and flags can clearly be seen on both sides of the esplanade in this image. The Chrysler Motors Building occupies a new wing extended to the left of the old Exposition Hall. Also visible around the circle in the upper right of this image are the U.S. Government Building, with its tower, and the Ford Motor Company Building. Facing the Ford Motor Company Building across the vast expanse of the Court of Honor is the Humble Oil Hall of Petroleum (far left of image). (Courtesy of the Dallas Historical Society Archives.)

The State of Texas Building was the most imposing structure on the fairgrounds. When it finally opened to fairgoers in September 1936, three months after the fair opened, it quickly became one of the most popular attractions at the exposition. The building's towering achievement was its incorporation of art as a propaganda vehicle to express the history, culture, and geography of Texas. An international team of artists was assembled to augment the building's classical modern architecture, a collaborative effort that produced some of the most splendid and awe-inspiring interior spaces in America. Former Texas governor Patt M. Neff described the building as "the Westminster Abbey of the Western World." (Courtesy of the Dallas Park and Recreation Department.)

In late 1935, construction was either well under way or would soon start on most the exposition's 77 new buildings. The single exception was the proposed exhibit building to be constructed as the centerpiece of the exposition by the state of Texas. When the consortium of 10 Dallas architecture firms hired by the State Board of Control failed to produce an acceptable design, George Dahl stepped in to remedy the increasingly desperate situation. He called in a young Houston architect named Donald Barthelme, who quickly produced a synthesis of the previous schemes and had it approved. His design for the State of Texas Building illustrates the influence of a famous Philadelphia architect, Paul Philippe Cret, whose classical modern aesthetic was abundantly applied in stone to the building's central exedra and flanking wings. (Courtesy of the Dallas Park and Recreation Department.)

At night, Fair Park was transformed into a pageant of lights and color that held the fair's visitors in awe. Along the esplanade, floodlights illuminated the pylons and sculpture and bathed the building facades with subtle shades of color. Following his similar success at the 1933 Century of Progress Exposition in Chicago, C. M. Cutler was the lighting engineer engaged by George Dahl to design the exposition's lighting system. Perhaps Cutler's greatest achievement in Dallas was the astounding fan of lights that emanated from behind the State of Texas Building each evening starting at 8:30 p.m. This array, which projected from a battery of 24 lights located directly behind the building, could easily be seen in Fort Worth, 30 miles west of Dallas, and as far away as Tyler, located 90 miles to the east. (Above, courtesy of the State Fair of Texas Archives; below, courtesy of the Dallas Municipal Archives.)

The Hall of State in the State of Texas Building presented visitors with a cathedral-like aura and grandeur amplified by the room's monumental size and proportions, the quality of its materials and finishes, and the seamless integration of its extraordinary artwork. Fluted columns of Texas Cordova stone supported a hand-stenciled ceiling from which bronze and aluminum tiered chandeliers were suspended. The Great Medallion of Texas was the focal point of the room. (Courtesy of the State Fair of Texas Archives.)

Two massive murals depicting Texas history on the side walls of the Hall of State were designed by Eugene Savage, an art professor at Yale University. When they were completed in 1936, these were reputedly the largest oil murals in the world. (Courtesy of the State Fair of Texas Archives.)

The Great Medallion was conceived by another Yale art teacher, Joseph Renier. In this immense, gilded bas-relief, a flood of rays emanating from the Lone Star bathed six symbolic figures, which continued the "six flags" theme initiated along the esplanade. In addition to their Yale connections, both Eugene Savage and Renier had previously won the prestigious Prix de Rome, in 1912 and 1915, respectively. (Courtesy of the State Fair of Texas Archives.)

The State of Texas Building featured additional exhibit rooms dedicated to the four geographic regions of the state. Each of these rooms depicted a specific region in the materials and detailing, images and iconography, and especially in the artwork. The East Texas Room featured walls paneled in East Texas gum and murals above the entrance doors painted by the Dallas artist Olin Travis. The pair of murals in this room was entitled *East Texas of Today, Before and After the Discovery of Oil*. In the above image, a majestic group of pine trees shelters the cotton and lumber interests of the region. In the foreground of this image, slumbering giants represent the potential of unimagined wealth and power hidden in the earth. The below image depicts East Texas after the discovery of the world's largest oil field in 1929. In this scene, the slumbering giants are awakening and ascending into the sky in the guise of black smoke from the oil field. Towering derricks, refinery smokestacks, and skyscrapers mark the rush of progress toward rapid industrialization and urbanization. This was an appropriate subject for a mural displayed in Dallas in 1936. Six years earlier, the discovery of the great East Texas Oil Field brought wealth and affluence to the city, and with it, the aspiration and means to stage a world's fair. (Both, courtesy of the State Fair of Texas Archives.)

The North Texas Room featured this fresco painting by Arthur Starr Niendorff, entitled *Old Man Texas.* The central figure was a cartoon character created by the *Dallas Morning News* in 1911 as the embodiment of citizenship in the state. In this highly representational image, the old man was used to symbolize the collective characteristics of the North Texas people—vitality, dynamism, and a love of the new and the modern. Old Man Texas is seen embracing the two skyscraper cities of the region, Fort Worth (left) and Dallas (right). On the left, a giant turbine symbolizes the growing industrial and manufacturing interests of North Texas; to the right, gold spills from the open door of a bank vault, symbolizing the large banking interests of the region. (Courtesy of the State Fair of Texas Archives.)

This view of the exposition, taken from the northeast, shows the large exhibit halls that flank the Esplanade of State and illustrates how the older state fair exhibit structures were incorporated into the design and layout of the Texas Centennial Exposition. To the left, a procession of vehicles passing by the Ford Motor Company Building can be seen entering the Court of Honor. (Courtesy of the Dallas Historical Society Archives.)

Huge crowds gather in front of the U.S. Government Building for a parade. The bas-relief at the base of the federal building can be seen in this image. A pair of federal medallions marks the two entrances to the building. On the right of this image is the long wall of the Ford Motor Company Building, and just beyond it, in the distance, is the Texaco Building. (Courtesy of the Dallas Historical Society Archives.)

The U.S. Government Building was designed by the chief architect on Dahl's staff, Donald Nelson. Nelson was recruited by Dahl from the 1933 Chicago fair, where he also designed the federal building at the Century of Progress Exposition. The U.S. Government Building was the tallest structure on the Texas Centennial Exposition grounds and marked its geographic center. The 179-foot-high tower, highlighted by gilded fluting on its leading edge and crowned by a stylized gold eagle designed by the artist Raoul Josset, stood in splendid, isolated contrast to the fair's predominantly horizontal sprawl. Along with the esplanade and State of Texas Building, the federal building became one of the Texas Centennial Exposition's memorable architectural icons. (Author's collection.)

The central rotunda of the U.S. Government Building ushered visitors into the main exhibit hall, where they could view exhibits of 30 different federal agencies. The rotunda featured four tall murals that depicted the geographic regions of the United States. Indirect lighting and a stenciled ceiling reinforced the vertical drama of this memorable space. (Courtesy of the Library of Congress.)

The Ford Motor Company Building and the U.S. Government Building are both prominent in this view. The Ford Motor Company Building featured a courtyard with covered outdoor dining and a performance stage. Across from this space, a series of paved and unpaved roads called Roads of the Southwest was built around the lagoon to give fairgoers an opportunity to ride in new Ford models on roads that simulated different driving conditions. To the right of the federal building and Ford Motor Company Building, Stadium Plaza provided a subtle cross-axis to the fairgrounds, visually connecting the entrance of the Cotton Bowl (above) across the lagoon to the Dallas Museum of Fine Arts (lower right). (Courtesy of the Dallas Historical Society Archives.)

The Ford Motor Company Building was by far the most expensive and elaborate of the privately built exhibit halls at the Texas Centennial Exposition. It was given a prominent site at the south end of the Court of Honor, where it had to contend with the 179-foot-high tower of the neighboring federal building. Detroit architect Albert Kahn and a prominent industrial designer from New York, Walter Dorwin Teague, collaborated on the design of this building, which featured a Streamline Moderne facade that was perhaps the most notable of any of the big exhibit structures at Fair Park. In 1937, the Ford Motor Company Building was renamed the Pan-American Exhibit Building for the Greater Texas and Pan-American Exposition, a repeat fair that followed the Texas Centennial Exposition. (Above, courtesy of the Texas/Dallas History and Archives Division, Dallas Public Library; below, author's collection.)

E-111 PATIO DE HONOR, SHOWING PAN-AMERICAN EXHIBIT BUILDING, PAN-AMERICAN EXPOSITION, DALLAS, 1937

Visitors entered the Ford Motor Company Building into a large semicircular lobby where various forms of transportation—from the horse-drawn carriage to the horseless carriage to the earliest Ford models—were displayed in a striking exhibit designed by Walter Dorwin Teague's office. (Courtesy of the Texas/Dallas History and Archives Division, Dallas Public Library.)

After passing through the lobby, visitors moved into a slightly smaller rotunda space, where they encountered a dramatic exhibit of Ford products utilized in the manufacture of its automobiles. In this image, the central display, dramatically lit by neon lighting, showcases the quantity of raw materials utilized by the manufacturer in its products each year. Additional raw materials were displayed around the perimeter wall. (Courtesy of the Texas/Dallas History and Archives Division, Dallas Public Library.)

Next, visitors encountered a long exhibit hall with displays organized along the two side walls. The circulation flow through the building was one way. The exit was through a landscaped courtyard on the building's south side, facing the lagoon and Roads of the Southwest, where rides in Ford automobiles were offered. (Courtesy of the Texas/Dallas History and Archives Division, Dallas Public Library.)

Exhibits in the Ford Motor Company Building included graphically compelling images and messages on the walls and well-organized displays of equipment and machinery utilized in the design and manufacturing processes of Ford automobiles. Live narrations and demonstrations, including scenic displays with actors, could be found throughout the exhibit hall. (Both, courtesy of the Texas/Dallas History and Archives Division, Dallas Public Library.)

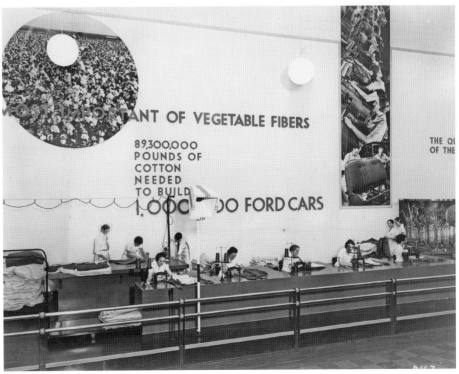

Directly opposite the courtyard and outdoor performance stage of the Ford Motor Company Building is Roads of the Southwest, where Ford cars could be test driven around the lagoon on a variety of surfaces simulating historic roads and routes of the southwestern United States and Central America. In the above image, three black sedans are parked, awaiting riders, while five more automobiles can be seen driving on the various roads. Above the lagoon, to the right of Stadium Plaza, is the Texaco Building, designed by Walter Dorwin Teague. In the image below, a new Ford sedan proceeds around the far side of the lagoon with the Ford Motor Company Building just visible through the trees on the right. (Both, courtesy of the Dallas Historical Society Archives.)

A Ford convertible is seen crossing a bridge on the lagoon on a segment of Roads of the Southwest. The Ford Motor Company Building is prominently visible in the distance of this image. In the image below, one of the six different roads built around the lagoon was the Pan-American Highway, which incongruously passed by the Forbidden City attraction on the lagoon's western shore. (Both, courtesy of the Texas/Dallas History and Archives Division, Dallas Public Library.)

The Fair Park Auditorium was converted to an automobile showroom and celebrity bandstand during the Texas Centennial Exposition. The fixed seating in the auditorium was removed and tiered platforms were constructed on the sloping floor to display automobiles. The Gulf Clouds fountain was relocated from its former location on a plaza inside the old state fair entrance gate to the front of the General Motors Building. To the left of the General Motors Building is the Hall of Negro Life. (Courtesy of the Dallas Historical Society Archives.)

During the Texas Centennial Exposition, many of the most renowned orchestras of the big band era played on the stage of the General Motors Building. The following year, the auditorium seating was restored and the building was renamed the Pan-American Casino during the Greater Texas and Pan-American Exposition of 1937. (Both, author's collection.)

The Hall of Negro Life, seen in the above image, was the first federally funded exhibit hall devoted to African Americans at a world's fair. In the below image, Texans could experience their first production of Shakespeare staged in a reproduction of the Globe Theatre, where four Shakespearean comedies and *Julius Caesar* were presented in repertory. (Above, courtesy of the Dallas Historical Society Archives; below, author's collection.)

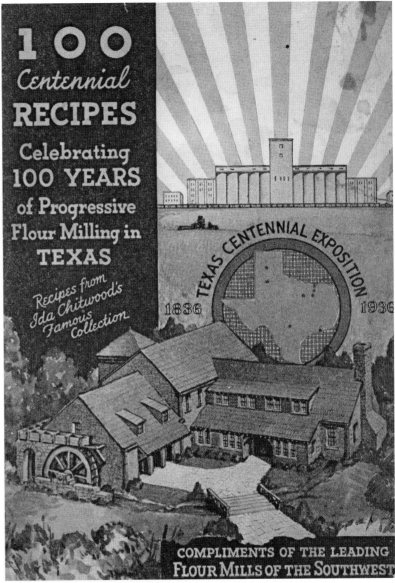

The vast majority of buildings at Fair Park were designed in the art deco or moderne style, including the Hall of Religion, seen here in the image at left. The Flour Milling Industry exhibit, illustrated at right on the cover of a Texas Centennial Exposition souvenir recipe book, had a rustic appearance in keeping with its "mill" theme. (Both, author's collection.)

The Magnolia Petroleum Building was one of several hospitality lounges built by oil companies at the Texas Centennial Exposition. It was designed by New York architect William Lescaze, whose rapid rise to fame occurred four years earlier when his work was included by Philip Johnson in the Museum of Modern Art exhibit on modern architecture. Lescaze was brought to Dallas by the city's famous fashion impresario Stanley Marcus, who wanted to see a truly "modern" building in his hometown—in contrast to the more stylized modernism that had been adopted by George Dahl as the predominant style at the exposition. This diminutive, avant-garde building introduced European modernism to Dallas in 1936. (Courtesy of the Dallas Historical Society Archives.)

In stark contrast to the Texaco Building was the Conoco Hospitality House, which eschewed the sleek, modern vocabulary of Teague's designs for the more familiar historical reference of Mount Vernon. (Courtesy of the Dallas Historical Society Archives.)

Hospitality lounges at the Texas Centennial Exposition provided fairgoers an opportunity to escape from the Texas heat and relax in air-conditioned comfort. Texaco and Conoco were two other petroleum companies with lounges—although in widely disparate styles. The Texaco Building, shown above, was designed by Walter Dorwin Teague, a celebrated industrial designer who was also largely responsible for the nearby Ford Motor Company Building. (Author's collection.)

Attendance at the Texas Centennial Exposition fell far short of the 10 million originally projected by fair organizers. Heat was one of the culprits, despite the air-conditioning available in the exhibit halls. The summer of 1936 was one of the hottest ever recorded in Dallas, with the temperature reaching 109 degrees in early August. The oppressive heat, coupled with the attire of the fashionable Dallas fairgoers evident in these two images, undoubtedly affected attendance. (Both, courtesy of the Dallas Historical Society Archives.)

The Rio Grande Valley exhibit consisted of a residence and outdoor garden squeezed into a leftover plot of land between other exhibit buildings. The Hall of Varied Industries looms in the background of this image. This building was originally constructed in 1922 as the Automobile and Manufacturers Building and was integrated by George Dahl into a much larger exhibit hall for the Texas Centennial Exposition. Unlike the buildings that bordered the esplanade, however, this particular facade did not receive a moderne face-lift. Its Spanish Revival elevation provided a suitable backdrop to the Rio Grande landscape. (Courtesy of the Dallas Historical Society Archives.)

The agriculture and livestock exhibits at the Texas Centennial Exposition were confined to the same area north of the stadium that they had occupied at state fairs since 1906. The existing barns and arena were re-skinned with simple moderne facades, and new exhibit halls and barns were designed by Dahl and his staff to augment the facilities. This was the first dedicated agrarian district at any world's fair. Entry into the section was between the monumental entrance porticoes of the Agriculture Building, seen at left of this image, and the Foods Building, on the right. Murals can be seen inside the porticoes of both buildings. (Courtesy of the Dallas Historical Society Archives.)

George Dahl's staff renovated existing structures and designed new livestock barns in the agrarian district to accommodate horses, cattle, swine, sheep, goats, and poultry. This image of the horse barn illustrates the elaborate and architecturally cohesive system of streetscaping devised for the exposition, consisting of lights, decorative pylons, street signs, and flagpoles seen here, which carried into the most remote areas of the fairgrounds. (Courtesy of the Dallas Historical Society Archives.)

Fair Park Stadium, built in 1930, was renamed the Cotton Bowl in 1936 and received new gatehouses and toilet buildings for the Texas Centennial Exposition. The pylons and concession building located in Stadium Plaza continued the simplified moderne detailing prevalent throughout Fair Park. (Courtesy of the Dallas Municipal Archives.)

The Century Café was located on the opposite side of the Cotton Bowl stadium, in the agrarian district. It was the largest freestanding restaurant at the Texas Centennial Exposition. (Author's collection.)

The *Cavalcade of Texas* was the hit of the exposition and an undertaking of immense magnitude. The 1934 racetrack grandstand provided seating in front of a spectacular outdoor stage, partially seen in the above image, which measured 300 feet by 170 feet. The $250,000 historical pageant had an average attendance of 8,000 at its nightly performances. (Both, courtesy of the Dallas Historical Society Archives.)

Mountains were fabricated to a height of 60 feet and acted as a backdrop to the elaborate sets, including a Spanish galleon and the Alamo, which were mounted on wheels and manually rolled on and off the stage during the 75-minute performance. Scenery changes were accomplished behind a 40-foot-high veil of water that rose from a pool and separated the spectators from the stage. (Author's collection.)

Pictured is a souvenir program for the *Cavalcade of Texas* at the Texas Centennial Exposition. (Author's collection.)

Dallas's bid for the Texas Centennial Exposition included a commitment of almost $8 million for land and permanent improvements, including buildings, streets, and other beautification work at the exposition site. Much of this investment was concentrated on new museums and cultural facilities that George Dahl grouped around a man-made lagoon, which was located on land purchased along Second Avenue. In this image, these facilities consisted of, counterclockwise from lower right, the Dallas Museum of Natural History, the Dallas Museum of Fine Arts, an open-air amphitheater, and the Hall of Horticulture. Located across from the amphitheater was a new aquarium. Not shown in this image is the Hall of Domestic Life, which was also a member of the cultural group. (Courtesy of the Dallas Historical Society Archives.)

City leaders envisioned the museums and facilities clustered around the lagoon as the cultural legacy of the Texas Centennial Exposition. In a single gesture, Dallas received the endowment of a substantial new civic center. The most important of these new buildings was the Dallas Museum of Fine Arts, which, like the State of Texas Building, was designed by a consortium of Dallas architects with guidance from the Philadelphia architect Paul Philippe Cret. This spartan building was designed in the classical modern style and clad in creamy limestone and Cordova stone. It was the centerpiece of the lagoon grouping and was on axis with the plaza and the entrance to the Cotton Bowl. (Courtesy of the Dallas Historical Society Archives.)

The open-air amphitheater seated 5,000 in a gently sloping bowl focused on the concentric rings of the band shell. It was designed by Scott Dunne, a noted theater designer in Dallas. (Author's collection.)

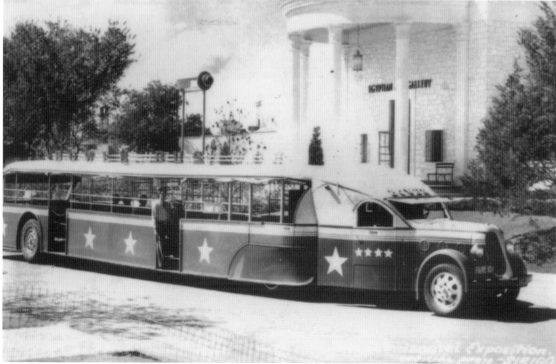

Other buildings in the cultural district surrounding the lagoon included an aquarium, as seen in the above image, and the Hall of Domestic Life, below. Transportation around the fairgrounds for hot and weary visitors was provided by 15 streamlined exposition coaches. In the image below, a coach is parked in front of the Hall of Domestic Life, awaiting passengers. (Above, author's collection; below, courtesy of the State Fair of Texas Archives.)

The National Cash Register exhibit recorded the daily attendance at the exposition with hourly updates. On the day this photograph was taken, the attendance had reached 45,379 by mid-afternoon. This exhibit was originally designed for Walter Dorwin Teague for the Century of Progress Exposition in Chicago three years earlier and was so popular that the company built a similar version of it in Dallas. (Courtesy of the Dallas Historical Society Archives.)

The Hall of Horticulture was highlighted by a sculptural bas-relief panel of Texas flora that ran across the base of the front facade of the building. A conservatory for the display of botanical specimens, seen on the right side of this image, had a south-facing glass wall and skylights. (Courtesy of the Dallas Historical Society Archives.)

Behind the Hall of Horticulture and across the street from the Hall of Domestic Life was an area of the exposition reserved for model homes. Model houses were among the most popular attractions at the Chicago fair and exposition organizers in Dallas made six lots available for construction product manufacturers to build on. These homes offered fairgoers the opportunity to evaluate new methods of residential construction and progressive concepts for interior comfort and convenience. Only four homes were built for the Texas Centennial Exposition, including the Contemporary Model Home, in the above image, and the Southern Pine House, below. These two houses represented the two extremes of mid-1930s residential design. The contemporary home was designed by the Dallas firm DeWitt and Washburn in the International style. By contrast, the Southern Pine House, designed by Goodwin and Tatum, represented the folksy charm that most fairgoers were familiar with. (Above, courtesy of the Dallas Park and Recreation Department; below, author's collection.)

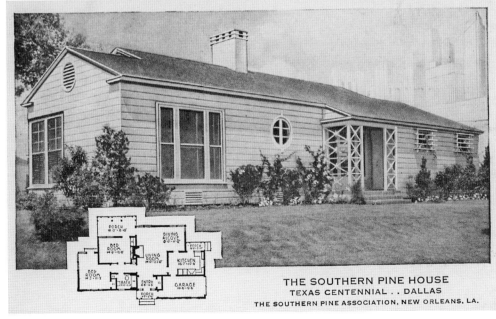

THE SOUTHERN PINE HOUSE
TEXAS CENTENNIAL . . DALLAS
THE SOUTHERN PINE ASSOCIATION, NEW ORLEANS, LA.

Near the model homes, in the farthest corner of the exposition grounds, the federal government built two exhibits side-by-side to showcase the National Park Service and the Works Progress Administration. Other nearby exhibits in this section of the fair included the Texas Ranger Station and a reproduction of the Alamo. The National Park Service exhibit was designed and constructed in conjunction with the Texas State Parks Board. It consisted of a typical cabin being built by the Civilian Conservation Corps (CCC) in state parks, seen in the above image, and an open-air structure for the display of exhibits, below. CCC enrollees from Paris State Park were dispatched to Dallas to construct the exhibit in a rustic style, using logs and rough lumber. (Both, courtesy of the National Park Service, Harper's Ferry Archives.)

The more colorful side of Texas history was depicted in this replica of Judge Roy Bean's saloon and courthouse, where he dispensed "Law West of the Pecos." Next door was an attraction called "The Moonshine Still." (Courtesy of the Texas/Dallas History and Archives Division, Dallas Public Library.)

In the lower left of this aerial view of Fair Park taken from the south, several model homes on the curving drive behind the Hall of Horticulture can be seen. The Contemporary Model Home and the Southern Pine House are both visible in this image, as is the Portland Cement House, to the left. Across the street from the homes is the Hall of Domestic Life, and above this the National Cash Register exhibit is visible. The midway is the long street stretching from the lower right of this image, to Stadium Plaza. (Courtesy of the Dallas Historical Society Archives.)

The midway at the Texas Centennial Exposition occupied a quarter-mile-long strip that extended from Stadium Plaza to the exposition boundary on Pennsylvania Avenue. It was lined with entertainment attractions, including the Streets of Paris seen in the center of this image, and educational exhibits such as Admiral Byrd's Little America, at the far left of this image, and Ripley's Believe It or Not, located across Cavalcade Drive to the right of Streets of Paris. Although the old state fair roller coaster was retained for the exposition, there were few rides on the midway. (Courtesy of the Dallas Historical Society Archives.)

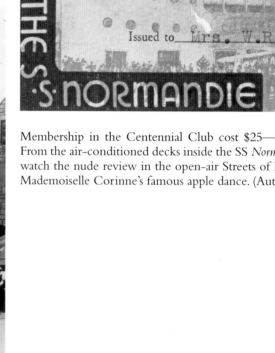

Membership in the Centennial Club cost $25—a significant sum in 1936. From the air-conditioned decks inside the SS *Normandie*, club members could watch the nude review in the open-air Streets of Paris below, highlighted by Mademoiselle Corinne's famous apple dance. (Author's collection.)

The reconstruction of familiar landmarks and historical and ethnic villages had been a favorite form of entertainment at fairs and expositions since the midway was first introduced at the World's Columbian Exposition in Chicago in 1893. During the 1930s, concessions and exhibits moved from one fair to the next, including the Streets of Paris, which was relocated to Dallas from the 1933 fair in Chicago. George Dahl designed a replica of the SS *Normandie*, which housed the Centennial Club on three air-conditioned "decks" overlooking the outdoor performance area of the Streets of Paris below. Venues like the Streets of Paris provided fair visitors with the experience of food, entertainment, and architecture of distant cultures. (Courtesy of the Texas/Dallas History and Archives Division, Dallas Public Library.)

The midway was a spectacular, quarter-mile-long pedestrian concourse with lavish entertainment venues, historical villages, educational exhibits, freak shows, and a few rides. George Dahl instilled a degree of order to this fantasy world with the design and installation of prominent and abstract lighting pylons along the entire length of the midway. (Courtesy of the Texas/Dallas History and Archives Division, Dallas Public Library.)

Admiral Byrd's Little America was a midway educational concession sponsored by D. Harold Byrd, a Dallas resident and cousin of the Antarctic explorer, Rear Adm. Richard E. Byrd. The attraction highlighted Admiral Byrd's highly publicized South Pole expedition and featured the explorer's airplane, *The Condor*, as well as a re-creation of his base camp. (Courtesy of the Texas/Dallas History and Archives Division, Dallas Public Library.)

In addition to the Streets of Paris, the midway featured several other foreign concessions and ethnic villages. These included the English Village, the Old Nuremburg restaurant, the City of China, the Streets of All Nations, and the $250,000 Black Forest concession, seen in this image with its elaborate gatehouse and clock tower facing the midway. Inside, paying customers could stroll through a replicated German village or enjoy an ice show on an outdoor skating rink while dining at the venue's 1,600-seat restaurant. (Author's collection.)

Crowds line up for the Hollywood Animal Show, which was one of the largest attractions on the midway. (Courtesy of the Texas/Dallas History and Archives Division, Dallas Public Library.)

Fairgoers assemble in droves for the matinee show at the Streets of Paris. On the left side of this image, across the midway from the Streets of Paris, is the Texas Showboat, and just beyond it, the front facade of the Holy City exhibit. Moderne light pylons march down the center of the pedestrian concourse toward the Gulf Oil Products exhibit, seen in the far distance. (Courtesy of the Texas/Dallas History and Archives Division, Dallas Public Library.)

The first artwork executed on the Texas Centennial Exposition grounds was located within the large *entrado* on the Hall of Administration. This concrete and plaster sculpture entitled *Spirit of the Centennial* was designed by Raoul Josset and carved by José Martin. Texas actress and singer Georgia Carroll modeled for Josset in this tribute to the builders of the exposition. She was a singer with the Kay Kyser band. The mural behind the sculpture was designed by Carlo Ciampaglia. (Author's collection.)

OPPOSITE: This photograph of the Court of Honor looking toward the Ford Motor Company Building illustrates the union of art, architecture, and landscape achieved by Texas Centennial Exposition planners and designers. (Courtesy of the Dallas Historical Society Archives.)

The Art of the Exposition

As the major buildings of the exposition neared completion, George Dahl and his chief architect, Donald Nelson, turned their attention to the exterior decoration. They brought to Dallas a group of mostly foreign-born artists they had met while studying in Europe during the 1920s. Several of these artists had also worked with Nelson at the Chicago Century of Progress Exposition in 1933. Their arrival in Dallas to work on the Texas Centennial Exposition was an economic windfall for the local artists who were employed by the exposition to assist in the execution of the murals, friezes, bas-reliefs, and sculpture at the fair.

However, the Dallas artists were not afforded any measurable degree of artistic freedom to participate in the design of the monumental exterior artwork and were essentially utilized as journeymen assistants. The interpretation of Texas history in the exposition's art program was therefore left to a group of artists totally unfamiliar with the state's history, traditions, and culture.

The murals painted on the buildings at Fair Park typically depicted the exhibit content found within. Carlo Ciampaglia's eight murals on the Hall of Transportation, for example, embodied a transportation theme, both historical and future.

The murals he designed for the Agriculture Building and Foods Building also depicted the exhibit content of those structures. All told, there were approximately two dozen monumental exterior murals created and an equal number of sculptures and bas-reliefs. Another large collection of murals and sculpture could be found in the interior spaces of the State of Texas Building and the U.S. Government Building. It was a remarkable output by a small but talented group of artists who assembled in Dallas in 1935 and 1936 to execute the artwork for the Texas Centennial Exposition.

George Dahl and his chief architect, Donald Nelson, assembled this large team of artists to design and execute the mural paintings, decorative painting, sculpture, and bas-reliefs at the exposition. The two architects met many of these artists in their prior travels and schooling in Europe. Nelson had also worked with several of the artists at the Century of Progress Exposition in Chicago and recommended them to Dahl. The major Texas Centennial Exposition artists visible in this image include Raoul Josset (first row on the left, with his thumbs in his belt), Carlo Ciampaglia (first row, center, with his left arm around the seated lady), Pierre Bourdelle (first row, right side, with his right arm around the seated gentleman), and Lawrence Tenney Stevens (upper row, left). Over 50 local artists were engaged by the exposition to assist in the execution of the art and in the decoration of the fairgrounds. (Courtesy of the Dallas Historical Society Archives.)

The Builders was a monumental mural seen in the above image of the west facade of the Hall of Varied Industries. It was designed by Pierre Bourdelle, son of the famed French sculptor Antonio Bourdelle. The artist was responsible for six other murals on this exhibit hall as well as a series of bas-reliefs on both this building and the Hall of Transportation. These bas-reliefs were created utilizing a similar technique to fresco painting, where layers of colored plaster were applied with a trowel and then shaped and carved into the final image while the plaster was still wet. In the below image, Bourdelle's *Man Taming Wild Horse* can be seen on the west facade of the Hall of Transportation. (Both, courtesy of the Dallas Historical Society Archives.)

53. Exhibit Building. Texas Centennial Exposition. OFFICIAL PHOTO – SIRIGO

Of the six monumental sculptures facing the esplanade, three were designed by Lawrence Tenney Stevens and three were designed by Raoul Josset, including his *United States,* seen in this image. Each 20-foot-high sculpture stood on a 12-foot pedestal base in front of a recessed arch, called an *entrado.* The portico behind the sculpture also contained monumental murals that depicted the theme of the exhibit hall. The murals in this image, *Electricity* on the left and *X-Ray* on the right, were designed by Pierre Bourdelle for the Hall of Electricity and Communications. (Author's collection.)

Sculpture could even be found in the livestock area of the exposition. *Texas Woofus* was designed by Lawrence Tenney Stevens, who went on to become the director of sculpture at the New York World's Fair in 1939. The chimerical figure was prominently positioned on a tall pedestal in front of Livestock Building No. 2. Executed in cast stone and chromium, it had the appearance of a pagan idol, composed of body parts from six different farm animals. (Courtesy of the Dallas Historical Society Archives.)

This scenic postcard image of the east end of the esplanade fountain shows a tall center pylon flanked by shorter sound pylons that concealed loudspeakers behind decorative grilles. In front of each sound pylon is a figural sculpture depicting "intangible sound." (Author's collection.)

The two sculptures *Tenor* and *Contralto* were designed by Lawrence Tenney Stevens. Stevens was responsible for the design of six sculptures at the Texas Centennial Exposition. (Both, courtesy of the Dallas Historical Society Archives.)

Carlo Ciampaglia was responsible for eight murals within the porticoes of the Hall of Transportation. Each of these murals depicted a mode or aspect of transportation, including *Navigation,* seen in this image. His semiclassical sweeping style was presented through the use of happy colors, for which he was noted among the other Texas Centennial Exposition artists. (Courtesy of the Dallas Historical Society Archives.)

This lunette mural by Carlo Ciampaglia was located over the entrance to the Poultry Building. (Courtesy of the Dallas Historical Society Archives.)

Ciampaglia also executed murals throughout the agrarian area, including monumental murals in the entrance porticoes of the Agriculture Building and Foods Building, in addition to smaller lunette murals at two other locations in the district. The murals on these buildings depicted agricultural and food themes, including *Goddess of the Harvest*, which was located above the entrance to the Foods Building. (Courtesy of the Dallas Historical Society Archives.)

Restoration of the former Hall of Transportation (now called the Centennial Building) was completed in 2000. Carlo Ciampaglia's eight murals on this building were restored in 2001. The six monumental sculptures in the esplanade, including Lawrence Tenney Stevens's *Texas*, seen in this image, were conserved in 2004. (Courtesy of Architexas.)

OPPOSITE: The esplanade fountain was reconstructed in 2009 at a cost of $12 million. The project included the re-creation of important missing elements removed sometime after the Texas Centennial Exposition. These items included the central pylon, seen in this image, and decorative light scoops that lined the edge of the pool. The *Tenor* and *Contralto* sculptures were also re-created and reinstalled in 2009. (Photograph by Carolyn Brown; courtesy of Quimby McCoy Preservation Architecture.)

FAIR PARK TODAY

In conjunction with Fair Park's centennial and its listing as a national historic landmark in 1986, the Dallas Park and Recreation Department initiated a capital improvement program that would increase Fair Park's viability as a year-round tourist destination and compliment the eight museums that were located on the fairgrounds. Initial work concentrated on vehicular circulation and parking, perimeter fencing, the re-creation of historic light fixtures, and the reconstruction of three porticoes on the south side of the esplanade that had burned in 1942.

Then, in the mid-1990s, a comprehensive restoration program was initiated, concentrating first on stabilizing the historic Texas Centennial Exposition buildings by addressing water infiltration and the replacement of obsolete and dangerous electrical systems. By the end of the decade, the Dallas Park and Recreation Department was able to initiate a more comprehensive program for the exterior restoration of Fair Park's architecture, a process that continues today. In addition, many of the public murals on the Texas Centennial Exposition buildings, which had been covered over with layers of paint, have been systematically uncovered, cleaned, and preserved. The remaining sculpture and bas-reliefs were similarly cleaned and conserved. Three of Lawrence Tenney Stevens's sculptures, which mysteriously vanished after the exposition, have been recreated and reinstalled in their original locations.

Since 1993, the City of Dallas and its private partners have reinvested over $200 million in Fair Park to preserve the legacy of the Texas Centennial Exposition as the last intact site from the moderne era of world's fairs in America.

The Agriculture Building (now known as the Food and Fiber Building) was restored in 1999. The murals were conserved in 2001. (Photograph by Charles Davis Smith, AIA; courtesy of Good Fulton and Farrell, Inc.)

Restoration of the exterior of the U.S. Government Building (now called the Tower Building) was completed in 2000. The exterior artwork, consisting of the bas–relief sculpture around the base of the building, the federal medallions above the entries, and the gold eagle atop the tower, were also conserved as part of this work. In 2002, the original exhibit hall was demolished and replaced with a near identical exhibit area with fire–proof construction and upgraded building systems. (Courtesy of the Dallas Park and Recreation Department.)

The Cotton Bowl was first expanded in 1948 and 1949 with the addition of upper decks on the east and west sides of the stadium. In 2008, the stadium was completely renovated and the seating capacity increased to 92,000 by extending the upper decks to form a continuous oval around the field. The stadium has been the site of the annual Red River Rivalry football game between the University of Texas and Oklahoma University since its completion in 1930. In 1960, the Cotton Bowl was the home of the Dallas Cowboys in the National Football League and the Dallas Texans (now the Kansas City Chiefs) in the American Football League. In 1994, the stadium hosted World Cup soccer matches. (Courtesy of the State Fair of Texas.)

The Hall of Administration was renovated in 2000 along with a major interior adaptive reuse as The Women's Museum. The mural and sculptures in front of the building were restored in 1998. (Photograph by Craig Blackmon, FAIA; courtesy of SmithGroup/F&S.)

The open-air amphitheater (now called the Bandshell) was restored in two phases culminating in 2002. (Courtesy of GSR–Andrade Architects.)

The Foods Building (now called the Embarcadero Building) was restored in 2005, including the rear lobby, seen in this image. (Photograph by Mark Knight; courtesy of Good Fulton and Farrell Architects.)

SELECTED BIBLIOGRAPHY

Breeze, Carla. *American Art Deco.* New York: W. W. Norton and Company, 2003.

Capitman, Barbara, Michael D. Kinerk, and Dennis W. Wilhelm. *Rediscovering Art Deco U.S.A.* Santa Monica: Hennessey and Ingalls, 2002.

Chariton, Wallace C. *Texas Centennial: The Parade of an Empire.* Plano, Texas: Privately printed, 1969.

Dillon, David. *Dallas Architecture 1936–1986.* Austin: Texas Monthly Press, 1985.

"Fairs." *Architectural Forum* (September 1936): 171–90.

Fuller, Larry Paul, ed. *The American Institute of Architects Guide to Dallas Architecture.* Dallas: American Institute of Architects, Dallas Chapter and McGraw-Hill Press, 1999.

McDonald, William L. *Dallas Rediscovered: A Photographic Chronicle of Urban Expansion 1870–1925.* Dallas: Dallas Historical Society, 1978.

Official Souvenir Guide: Texas Centennial Exposition. Dallas: Texas Centennial Central Exposition, 1936.

Ragsdale, Kenneth B. *The Year America Discovered Texas: Centennial '36.* College Station: Texas A&M University Press, 1987.

Rucker, Harry. "The Magic Touch of Illumination: The Illumination of the Esplanade of State at the Texas Centennial Exposition, Dallas—1936." Collection of Willis Winters, 1996. Photocopy.

Rydell, Robert W. *World of Fairs: The Century-of-Progress Expositions.* Chicago: University of Chicago Press, 1993.

Speck, Lawrence W. *Landmarks of Texas Architecture.* Austin: University of Texas Press, 1986.

"Texas Centennial Exposition." *Architectural Forum* (July 1936): 9, 62.

Texas Centennial In Pictures: The Official Souvenir View Book of the Texas Centennial Exposition, Dallas. Dallas: John Sirigo, 1936.

"Texas Has Its Centennial." *Pencil Points* (February 1936): 60–66.

Wiley, Nancy. *The Great State Fair of Texas.* Dallas: Taylor Publishing Company, 1985.

Winters, Willis. "Planning the Centennial." *Texas Architect* (May-June 1999): 54–61.

———. "The Architecture of the Dallas Fairs 1886-1936." Research paper, University of Texas at Austin, 1979.

www.arcadiapublishing.com

Discover books about the town where you grew up, the cities where your friends and families live, the town where your parents met, or even that retirement spot you've been dreaming about. Our Web site provides history lovers with exclusive deals, advanced notification about new titles, e-mail alerts of author events, and much more.

MADE IN THE USA

Arcadia Publishing, the leading local history publisher in the United States, is committed to making history accessible and meaningful through publishing books that celebrate and preserve the heritage of America's people and places. Consistent with our mission to preserve history on a local level, this book was printed in South Carolina on American-made paper and manufactured entirely in the United States.

This book carries the accredited Forest Stewardship Council (FSC) label and is printed on 100 percent FSC-certified paper. Products carrying the FSC label are independently certified to assure consumers that they come from forests that are managed to meet the social, economic, and ecological needs of present and future generations.

FSC
Mixed Sources
Product group from well-managed forests and other controlled sources

Cert no. SW-COC-001530
www.fsc.org
© 1996 Forest Stewardship Council

Find Your Place in History.